AMPLITUDE

By the same author:

Books:
Henderskelfe (with photographs of Castle Howard by Peter Heaton)
Asterisk (with photographs of Shandy Hall by Marion Frith)
Analogue/Digital: New & Selected Poems
The Bulmer Murder
Chromatic

Chapbooks:
Keys; Fire; Orange; Rhyme; Sound; The Music Lovers; Iron Age

As editor:
Reading the Applause (with Stephen Wade)
Feeling the Pressure: Poetry and science of climate change
Strange Cargo: Five Australian Poets
Tract: Prose poems (with Monica Carroll)
Metamorphic: 21st century poets respond to Ovid (with Nessa O'Mahony)
Abstractions (with Shane Strange)
Giant Steps (with Shane Strange)
No News (with Shane Strange and Alvin Pang)
Divining Dante (with Nessa O'Mahony)

Screenplay:
The Darkroom (with Kit Monkman, Thomas Mattinson, Hettie Shirazu)

AMPLITUDE

PAUL MUNDEN

RECENT
WORK
PRESS

Amplitude
Recent Work Press
Canberra, Australia

Copyright © Paul Munden, 2022

ISBN: 9780645356335 (paperback)

A catalogue record for this
book is available from the
National Library of Australia

Cover image: Underwater photograph © Fiona Edmonds Dobrijevich, combined with the author's surviving Yamaha CS–5 synthesizer. Reproduced with permission.
Cover design: Recent Work Press and Paul Munden
Set by Recent Work Press

recentworkpress.com

Contents

POEMS FOR STRINGS

SIGHT-READING: LA SERENISSIMA

INTERMEZZO: AUSTRALIA

THE ART OF NOISE

THE ROMANTICS

REPRISE

x	=	oscillating variable
A	=	amplitude
ω	=	angular frequency
t	=	time
K	=	arbitrary constant representing time offset
b	=	arbitrary constant representing displacement offset

POEMS FOR STRINGS

My soul, a stringed instrument, sang to itself, invisibly touched
—Friedrich Nietzsche

> *the cry of the strings,*
> *the cry of the mind,*
> *under the rosined bow.*
—Ellen Bryant Voigt

Baroque

It's mostly planned
around the company, the wine.
Very occasionally, one string will snap
but tonight as I tune up, tuck
the violin under my chin

and twist my hand
into position, it's my rup-
turing tendon that will make
us—before we've even started—stop.

'Greensleeves'

I'm put on hold
and one of a handful
of inevitable tunes
kicks in to accompany
my sigh: 'easy listening'
that's not easy at all
when compulsory

      and relayed
      with the tinny overtones
      of some cheap hearing aid.
      So while it drones
      I call up a contrasting
      memory, a hush,
      as I walk

along a quiet
wooded avenue until
I see him—
across a manicured lawn—
sitting at his grand
piano in the window,
deep in thought,

      writing one
      of his trademark
      arrangements with cascading
      strings, lush
      as the garden blending
      into the tall pine
      trees beyond...

I don't want Mantovani
said McCartney
when George Martin
suggested a quartet
for 'Yesterday'. And yet,
I do—I want that sensory
fill, that startling stereo-

       phonic effect of time
       to keep monotony
       at bay, the calm, green
       harmonics of space;
       to be that ten-year-old
       boy, looking in
       to where music takes place.

A Gift

for Anouska

The violin perched, slack-
strung, on the dark
wooden sideboard
of your Palermitan apartment
opposite the cathedral;
a gift you didn't yet know
how to tune, let alone play.

> Your guests ignored it,
> heading straight for the plates
> of cheese, olives, bread,
> and plastic flagons
> of wine
> from the market, music
> flowing from an amplified phone.

Smokers braved the narrow
stone balcony high
above the lines of traffic—
chains of lights
crawling between
Porta Nuova and the sea.
On the clocktower, pigeons

> became gargoyle silhouettes.
> The occasional miniature dog
> was lowered in a basket
> on a creaking pulley
> to the pavement
> for relief.
> I wondered what else

I had failed to teach you,
and if that mattered,
watching you thread
the multilingual
party with such intuitive skill
while I,
tongue-tied,

       retreated
       with the dumb instrument,
       turning each stiff
       peg
       until the new-
       ly levelled strings could be
       quietly at ease.

Enfant Terrible

During her lessons, a small boy sits under the grand piano, an outlaw hiding in the shade of a dark tree, happily doing nothing but watch the girl's bare legs with their white ankle socks and buckled blue shoes, dangling, his mother's in stockings that cling to her plump white thighs. He listens to the tentative, repetitive mistakes, and then—when his mother takes charge—the full power of the music in the canopy overhead: the boom of the tingling strings; the sheriff's posse on the gallop.

*

He can still hear his mother's muffled ground floor piano as he whiles away hours in the attic bedroom. On tiptoe he can see the blank horizon beyond the pier. A platypus and koala keep company in the corner—gifts from the father he has never met, who plays the cello, and is drinking himself to death under a harsh southern sun on the far side of the world. This year's gift is more compelling: a train set that has taken no time to assemble—the track articulating the confines of his frustrated, five-year-old life. Longer, by far, is the time he takes to pull the wings and all but two legs from a fly and position the awkward, homemade driver in the engine cab. Now he watches the whole ensemble glide around the room, resting his chin on the waxed pine boards, his eyes level with the empty carriages reflecting in the gleam.

*

The improvised breaks were already out of hand, but now the bow begins to thrash against the strings, its flayed filaments drifting in a haze of rosinous dust, a savagery fuelled by Polish spirit, stretching the music to the point that it must surely snap... it hangs by a shred, the spot-lit figure writhing on the floor, the violin somehow still gripped between shoulder and chin, the bow finding space to do more damage, and as we hold our breath in the dark, there's a moment of calm, which could almost be mistaken for defeat, the end, but it's the silence in which everything turns—a twitch upon the thread—and we watch the crumpled figure uncurl, the music cradled after all, brought back from the brink, tiny gasps of melody feeling their way before hurtling towards relief.

*

He looks for somewhere to place the Lafont Guarneri del Gesù once owned by Adolf Brodsky, and chooses the open grand at which Janusz Olejnicak is taking his seat, and you think surely not... The varnish on this fiddle is no mere gloss; its layers embody the history of its play, the ever-richening tone of a performative life, heritage made audible. And now he's looking for somewhere to put his bottle of beer, and you think please please God no...

The Four Seasons

for Nigel Kennedy and the Orchestra of Life

Spring (E Major: allegro—largo—allegro)

Ushered in by a noodling guitarist,
the birds are in full swing; for the soloist,
with this music in his veins, it's a lark.
In his Villa shirt he chirps and chirrups
as tight, bright buds unfurl to improvise
a canopy of leaves. His supple wrist
whips up a storm then settles for reprise.

> A trance... he drifts off—sprawled under the trees
> among daisies and meadow buttercups—
> to a sampled, softly murmuring breeze
> and the viola's monotonous bark.

Bring on the cheerleaders, goat skins and pipes,
revelry that breaks into yelps and whoops...
The dogs are out—Yeah! A bump of the fist.

Summer (G Minor: allegro non molto—adagio—presto)

Scorched pines. A sweltering stasis. The heat
has pressed the air almost to silence. Note
follows note like stuttering beads of sweat
but there—in the bow's quick tilt—the cuckoo,
followed by a warbling dove and the trill
of the finch, those fingers thrillingly close.
Breezing triplets flutter against a beat
the north wind blasts to hell—and there'll be more.

      A fly-infested lull—a fractious growl
      that's shorthand for a livewire scare. Why not—
      with a stack of Marshalls to hand—let loose

the thunder and lightning for real? ... One ... two
mississippi three mississippi four ...
The cornfields are all trashed by golf-ball hail.

Autumn (F Major: allegro—adagio molto—allegro)

Jazz trumpet? It's a party!—the harvest
gathered in. The drinking is in earnest
with flagons of claret and ale on tap;
they drink at the gallop, drink till they drop,
nod off ... only to get that second wind
and party on full pelt into the night.

      Passed out, they enter a parallel realm—
      a kaleidoscopic haze in which time
      is an elasticated, weightless dream
      in the autumnal cool—sleeping till dawn

when it's hip flask, hunting horn, horse and hound.
One poor terrified animal must run
for its life—their sport. It gives up the fight.
Sling it over a saddle and trot home.

Winter (F Minor: allegro non molto—largo—allegro)

Frost... snow... layers of ice. The wind has bite.
We're shivering in its grip, a cold snap
like nothing we've known... brrrrrr... We run and thump
our numbed, gloved hands together, stop and stamp
our snow-deep frozen boots on frozen earth.

> Later, feet up, in a chair by the hearth,
> I hear the pizzicato rain outside,
> a soporific, intimate reprieve

before we're back on the shifting ice, slide
and slip with skittering strings that believe
they can negotiate the cracks. The slap-
stick of our fall is what hurries our flight,
and if the wind howls through the house despite
battening it down, it's a shrill delight.

Fractious

He was meant to be playing the Elgar concerto with Leonard Slatkin but changed his mind a few weeks ago...
—Norman LeBrecht, 4 May 2016

He had an injury to his left hand and the Elgar was simply not comfortable physically at this time. All of us are thrilled to have him back, no matter what he is playing.
—Leonard Slatkin, 4 May 2016

I would rather have my prostate removed instead of listening to him play his own piece of music.
—'Ivan', 4 May 2016

I attended the concert, which was fabulous. One standing ovation after another.
—Stephen Calkins, 8 May 2016

from *Slipped Disc* (slippedisc.com)

For Elgar, read Ellington. A twinge in the arm. A new reality you have to accept. If the cartilage scrapes, so might the bow. You drink to ease the pain and remember the drink that made you fall. For Ellington, read Elgar. What might have been niggles like a flickering of bone.

For Ellington, read Elgar. A twinge in reality. A new drink you have to accept. If the arm scrapes, so might the bone. You drink to ease the Ellington and remember the Elgar that made you fall. For cartilage, read pain. What might have been niggles like a flickering of the bow.

For Elgar, read pain. A twinge in the bone. A new bow you have to accept. If the Ellington scrapes, so might the cartilage. You drink to ease the Elgar and remember the Ellington that made you fall. For drink, read reality. What might have been niggles like a flickering of the arm.

For Elgar, read drink. Ellington in the bow. A new cartilage you have to accept. If the bone scrapes, so might the Ellington. You drink to ease reality and remember the twinge that made you fall. For pain, read arm. What might have been niggles like a flickering of Elgar.

For Elgar, read arm. A flickering of pain. A new Ellington you have to accept. If reality scrapes, so might the twinge. You drink to ease the cartilage and remember the bow that made you fall. For Ellington, read Elgar. What might have been niggles like a drink of bone.

For Elgar, read cartilage. A twinge in the bow. A new arm you have to accept. If the flickering scrapes, so might the drink. You drink to ease the Ellington and remember the pain that made you fall. For Elgar, read bone. What might have been niggles like an Ellington of reality.

For Elgar, read Elgar. A twinge of pain. A new flickering you have to accept. If the cartilage scrapes, so might the reality. You drink to ease the drink and remember the arm that made you fall. For Ellington, read Ellington. What might have been niggles like a bow of bone.

For Elgar, read reality. A twinge of Ellington. A new Elgar you have to accept. If the bow scrapes, so might the pain. You drink to ease the bone and remember the cartilage that made you fall. For arm, read Ellington. What might have been niggles like a flickering of drink.

Duet

A two-man crosscut saw
rips its brusque path
through the sprawl
of an ancient sycamore
in the Craiglockhart garden
where Owen and Sassoon
spent shell-shocked leave.

It's a standard operation,
midwinter, before the sap
starts to rise—
a judicious sacrifice
for the benefit of the tree—
the heavy limb
roped, then slowly cradled

to the ground. Split,
its dense pages fall
open like a book:
one, for the younger man,
to be worked from sup-
ple greenwood in defiance
of traditional technique;

the other must wait
until seasoned—fit
to capture a darker tone—
when the luthier's steel
will once more nurse
mute wood's recuperation
into song. Now they form

a new alliance
as comrades in peace—
two violins unburden-
ing the tumultuous years
within their shared
and sculpted grain—
even as the world

        tilts ever again
        towards the pitiful wrath
        of war—bleak
        underscore
        to the melodic weave
        of what is spared,
        incumbent, but free.

Three-Part Invention

for Lizzy

You surprised me, first
by moving in
to this sleepy village
nestling above
the Vale of York
in the Howardian Hills,
then with the pastime

       you'd let drop,
       like me: the violin.
       I wondered
       if I might write—
       and we might play—
       some simple two-part
       invention by way

of restoring
mutual skills.
And while a theme
of sorts took shape
oh so slowly in my head,
I saw you forge
on with your work

       of creating a home.
       How could I not love
       the verve
       with which you pursued
       your dream
       as I once did mine,
       digging a trench,

filling one skip
after another, preparing
a garden—the music
in further counterpoint
now with the past,
too complex to perform
or even notate.

        These co-productive
        words, instead,
        must serve
        to convey the joint
        yet incomplete
        endeavour; the pledge;
        the imaginative leap.

SIGHT-READING:
LA SERENISSIMA

When I seek another word for 'music',
I never find any other word than 'Venice'.
—Friedrich Nietzsche

we're almost at those public gardens where they hold the Biennale ...
We may lose our way. It's not very well lit.
—Daphne du Maurier, 'Don't Look Now'

One morning

I wake as my daughter
pounds along
the landing
to my bedroom,
troubled by her dream—

Daddy! Is there a place
with streets made of water?—
her searching face
its own fabulous kingdom.

A Prima Vista

for Lara

That first night
we set off after dinner
on a meandering trek
from the Al Sole hotel
to the Rialto, a little
worried about
finding our way back

       but we came up
       with a plan—commit
       to memory each passing
       feature: the antique shop
       on the corner;
       that turquoise
       blouse

hanging
from a balcony...
and because
we were both struck
by different things, our make-
shift collaborative map
enabled us

       to retrace each step
       through the maze
       of *calli* and *sotoporteghi*.
       Like playing a new duet,
       by sight, side
       by side, the trick
       was to keep

moving, albeit
slightly slow, to look
ahead ahead
of time, and avoid
the dead
ends that would
defeat us. Alone we might

      have faltered, failed;
      together, we held
      our nerve—we knew
      enough from our one,
      careful, dual scan
      of the city's notation
      to make it through.

Don't look now

but the blond-haired girl in the bright red plastic mac is about to lose her red ball in the pond; she pulls the cord on her Action Man doll, and the mechanical voice is that of the elderly, psychic twin who, later, in Venice, will claim to have seen her still alive; the piano music hesitates, childlike, so that we somehow hear the fulfilment of each phrase before it sounds; inside, by the fire, the girl's father is looking through slides, confused by a red-hooded figure in the corner of a church; suddenly the girl is a running reflection of what we will see in a Venetian canal; her brother cycles over a pane of glass—the crack pre-echoing the crash of a timber through glass above the father's head that will leave him hanging; and it's now that she throws her ball into the pond, as a packet of cigarettes is tossed across the room from husband to wife; a drink tips over onto the slide and rocks with the same lilt as the ball on the water, as red begins to seep across the photographed church, and already the brother's desperate call is going unheard but we know, like the father, that the girl is drowning and his task is to haul her from the pond... and still the colour seeps across the slide, pre-figuring blood from his own neck; his wife's scream turns to a power-drill drilling a Venetian stone church wall...

Sonnetini Veneziani

Outside the main doors

of the Art Biennale
I don't give too much
thought to the assembly
of pigeons overhead.
Only inside

with dozens of silent, static
pigeons all around, do I finally
realise how I'm such
a poor critic.

(Biennale 2011, Giardini)

In a Palazzo

off the beaten track,
someone is playing Bach
on a Steinway adorned
with Maori carvings, lacquered in red.
In the garden at the back,

two massive, black, horned
bulls on top of standard black
pianos keep a firm lid
on further sound.

(Michael Parekowhai, *On first Looking into Chapman's Homer*, Palazzo Loredan dell'Ambasciatore, Biennale 2011, New Zealand Pavilion)

In the San Giorgio Basilica

they have allowed Anish Kapoor
to engineer his dream:
Ascension, a column
of smoke rising from a drum
in the aisle, and carrying our

gaze slowly upward to where—
in a steel duct placed in the dome—
it is spirited away; prayer
made visible in material air.

(Biennale 2011, Basilica di San Giorgio Maggiore)

In the Palladian Refectory

where the original once hung,
a perfect digital reconstruction
of Veronese's Canan wedding
comes to life. And yes, Jesus
is in the thick of it, as are we, whis-

pered conversation in our ears, as
Greenaway's genius
turns not only water into wine,
but the weather on canvas into rain.

(*Veronese, Le Nozze di Cana, a Vision by Peter Greenaway,*
Biennale 2009, Palladian Refectory, Isola di San Giorgio
Maggiore)

Inside one hall

of the curated pavilion
and nestling within
a dedicated wall
of intricate, hinged cabinets
comprised of individual

compartments—a collection
of miniature, imaginary beasts,
carved from wood, pale
as embryonic thoughts.

(Biennale 2013, Giardini)

In the Gaggiandre

the city's flood warning system
has been scored for full alarm,
the shipyards the auditorium
in which we can experience
the sound of catastrophe,

but the technology
has failed: there's an eerie
silence—
a pre-echo of post-apocalypse calm.

(Tomás Saraceno, *Acqua Alta: En Clave de Sol*, Biennale
2019, Arsenale)

In the British Pavilion

an enormous, furious
William Morris
hurls an oligarch's yacht
into the lagoon. What's not
to like, as we bear witness

with cups of tea, and make
our own woodblock
prints of the scene: tourists
cum artists.

(Jeremy Deller, *English Magic*, Biennale 2013, Giardini)

In a sunlit home from home

sixteen giant tortoises
cast from fibreglass resin
have been flown in
from the Seychelles; domed canvases
on which a matching creep

of humankind has come up
with a childlike, colourful
plea—under the auspices
of art—that we dawdle here awhile.

(Group Sez, *Slowly, Quietly,* Biennale 2017, Giardini
della Marinaressa)

In Paradiso

on the Giardini waterfront,
as the sun sinks low,
we sit with a beer or aperol
spritz in hand, our feet
having taken the brunt

of the ordeal—
of which tomorrow
will be a close repeat
with indefatigable appeal.

(Biennale (n.d.), Giardini)

Wrong Way Time

It's a special form
of purgatory, so many
defaced clocks
rubbing spotlit
shoulders in the dark,
decommissioned into art.
There are pendulum

       swings, but they're
       random—
       the relentless ticks
       competing, like
       a quiet cacophony
       of beetles or book lice
       erasing edible word

after word.
It's the new Australian
Venice Pavilion,
and I'm used to the idea
of *there* and *here*,
just as I am
with *now* and *then*,

       but this is different,
       a dysfunctioning shock.
       Grandfathers are skeletons,
       decorative coffins
       inside out—
       we don't see the workings
       just the markings—

childlike bones
painted on the long case,
a skull on the face.
A QR code
gives a cuckoo clock
a ghoulish look
that seems to proclaim

　　　how summertime
　　　will burst
　　　forth at the worst
　　　possible moment.
　　　The odd, crude slogan
　　　is a help for anyone
　　　in doubt.

(Fiona Hall, *Wrong Way Time*, Biennale 2015,
Australian Pavilion)

From *The Wreck of the Unbelievable*

Damien Hirst, Venice, 9.IV–3.XII.2017

nunc quoque curaliis eadem natura remansit,
duritiam tacto capiant ut ab aere quodque
*vimen in aequore erat, fiat super aequora saxum.**
      —Ovid, *Metamorphoses*, Book IV

those are pearls that were his eyes
      —Shakespeare>Eliot

1. Punta della Dogana

Poacher turned gamekeeper, Hirst-Cerberus,
has wormed his way into the customs house
as faux guardian of these waterways,
hauled—from the deep—Ovidian treasures
while filming the whole charade: Proteus
in coral-encrusted bronze; a tortoise
cast in silver and gold; a mutant mouse
on the limestone foot of a colossus;
and a woman whose cling-wrapped body has,
for a head, the compound loudspeaker eyes
of a gargantuan fly. She's speechless
(like me), struggling—as the back of her dress
is breached by arthropoid legs—to process
the conceit: *Somewhere between truth and lies*

2. Palazzo Grassi

lies the truth. Here the coral has its hold
on toy Transformers; Spielberg's puppet shark
is gunning for Andromeda, SeaWorld
the logo glimpsed on a sword as your laugh
twists to a loss adjuster's casual grin.

Then I see the snakes of Medusa's hair,
carved out of malachite, and imagine
how labourers, doing his dirty work—
chipping poisonous dust into the air—
hoped their contributory craft might morph

into genuine art. His sketches bear
an anagram signature: *in this dream ...*
I'm telling all this as if I was there,
and perhaps I was. What have I become?

* *Even now corals have the same nature, hardening at a touch of air, and
what was alive, under the water, above water is turned to stone.*

L'Ospedale della Pietà

Once upon a time
these ornate iron grilles
high in the church walls
kept teenage girls
away from any prurient gaze—
or worse.
Today, it's the reverse:

> they help us visualise
> the *figlie* whose
> fairytale ability—
> amongst the discarded
> children of the poor
> and the bastard offspring
> of the nobility—

turned them into stars.
There's a small hatch
through which
the holy sacrament
could be passed.
A guide unlocks the door
to a narrow staircase

> and I follow to where
> I can see precisely how
> Antonio Lucio Vivaldi—
> Red Priest—
> could be more
> than mere voyeur.
> There's a meticulous list

of every foundling,
every instrument
in the maestro's care,
and the elaborate lace
worked by those
not chosen for
orchestra or choir;

       such virtuosic power,
       that even now
       the unguarded
       listener might become
       some kind of beast,
       transported, giddy
       with vicarious desire.

Encore

Five hundred concerti,
maybe more, or—
as at least one critic claims—
just the one,
re-written

five hundred times.
Words within the score
distinguish just four,
securing their immortality.

Glass Harp

On the corner of the square an elderly Venetian had set up stall with his glass harp: wine glasses filled to different depths, so that when he ran his moist fingers across the various mouths, they would each produce their singular note—and together, a clear-voiced harmony that carried to where we sat with our bellinis, eating blue cheese crostini. His quick looping hands conjured Vivaldi (his breaths the fleeting dips of his fingers into water) even as the waiter was carrying a Quattro Stagione to our table, the music held in the evening air. And when, years later, although the man on the corner had gone, we sat in the same square and the same waiter brought us a menu that hadn't changed, and raised our glasses—mine half empty, yours half full, G♭, F♯—his clear movements still reflected there, ringing in our ears.

An elasticated web

stretches between four
walls, ceiling and floor.
You pluck one rubber wire
on the far side of the room—
which might also be the world—

and I feel the vibration sing
in my fingers that hold
a different part of something
that might also be a poem.

(Tomás Saraceno, *Galaxy forming along
filaments, like droplets along the strands of a
spider's web*, Biennale 2009, Giardini)

INTERMEZZO: AUSTRALIA

Being lost in Australia gives you a lovely sense of security.
—Bruce Chatwin, *The Songlines*

It's the biggest open-air museum in the world.
—BeeLoved City

I overhear

the tumble of dried fruit—cherries, currants, raisins, sultanas—and
the rest is imagined: cinnamon, the grated rind of an orange,
sifted flour... then there's a crack—'never mind, let's try another!'—
and I picture the smashed yolk wiped from the floor before the
comic repeat, but I forge on with my own task, and later let a
quarter bottle of cognac weep into a heavy brass punchbowl,
watching the drenched slices of fruit submerge then reappear as
I wait for the first guests; and what I see, deep within the ripples
of Christmases past, is the future: tannin stained streams as I walk
through the bush, and two crocodiles thrashing in a tinted river,
glimpsed from the top of the gorge.

Relocation

It comes
with an allowance
and I'm daft enough
to use it. I take
the essentials: clothes,
violin, some restraint—
an old electric

      keyboard, not a piano—
      and familiar treasures
      to make myself
      at home:
      a few pictures,
      a roomful of poetry,
      and as a whim-

sical experiment
my father's
desk—I want to see
what the past looks like
once it's travelled
across the world.
But I get there

      ahead of it,
      and spend the night
      in an empty apartment
      while customs
      rummage and re-
      pack so lazily that
      my mother's tea set

quickly translates
into dust. My life
oscillates
for three years
between hemispheres,
allegiance
stretched to the limit

> and beyond
> and still the end
> is nowhere in sight.
> I can't know
> the news that awaits;
> the utterly random
> shock.

I walk alone

through what's already familiar bush, alert to the birds: crimson
and eastern rosellas, galahs, noisy miners and sulphur-crested
cockatoos—one inching sideways along the bare line of a branch
to snuggle with its mate. Rainbow lorikeets, way up within the
foliage, shine by virtue of their orange breasts. Camouflaged in
the grass, a pair of red rumped parrots takes off almost from under
my feet. I watch their swift, harmonious glide through the trees,
the subtly modulated greens.

#Bestiary

lift the toilet seat
and there's the little frog,
happy as Larry

*

lounging by the pool,
the resident perentie, his torn
side clawed by an eagle

*

in my mouth, my ears
and in the tears in the corner
of my eyes: flies

*

on cue for their photo call,
wild dolphins all known
to the rangers by name

*

a miniature hang-glider
lands awkardly on the beach—
again, again! pelican!

*

loping round the carpark,
a dingo on his forensic mission
pretending to be lost

*

on open ground
sticks and shadows conspire
to conceal an echidna

*

dusk, and from nowhere
the dreadful thud
of cow into car

With daily practice

my stiff fingers found
a music of their own,
the muscle memory of my arm
a rhythm akin
to the unique routine

of a bird of paradise,
waiting for you to come
to my patch of ground
and allow me to impress.

An Artist's Studio

for Fiona

You stand in the sweat-
box of your studio, glazed.
The concrete floor
is a layered spatter
of paint
from the days
you could still hold

        a brush in your limp
        wet hand. Paint oozes
        from fat aluminium
        tubes—paint like butter
        that unclouds, loses
        its emulsified tint
        and disappears

into the grain
of what, today, is too hot
to eat. Cold beers
from the thundering fridge
will only make you more
thirsty. The industrial fan
struggles to create

        the illusion of a breeze;
        air more like a clamp.
        Wasps don't know
        what's hit them, each
        curled
        like a devilish embryo
        on the windowsill,

cradling its death,
the sweltering studio
now a morgue—
the very thought
of making art here
utterly inert,
an undepictable lull

before the random,
rogue,
bone-numbing ice-storm
to come—the freeze
that will take your breath
and force you to witness it
unravelling, useless, erased.

(Sydney, Spring 2019)

Orange

Of all the new purchases filling your basket, I sensed your favourite was the fist-sized tube of neon orange—an impulse, an excitement among the necessary supplies—so that now I picture it in pride of place on your workbench with all those colours of the sea, your hand straying towards it with a sudden highlight in mind, and before I know it I am squeezing a thick bright splurge from the metal tube onto your palette, daubing an intrusive *me me me* on your thoughts.

*

I remember the oranges in the back of the car, driving down from Kurrajong, a plastic mesh bagful, like overweight tennis balls, thrown among the clutter—paints, brushes, towels, shoes—and haul them into my lap, at which you break from your thoughts and nod, eagerly, as I rip into the bag with mirrored fists, and pass one, watching you bite across its top, and begin to peel a long, single curl from the pith, resting your hand on the steering wheel, which makes me take it back and finish the job—'in one piece!' you insist—before I tear the fruit into rough segments and feed them to you as you drive, watching you devour them, more thirsty than hungry, and when you ask for another I happily oblige, smiling into the unreadable blue haze.

*

When I see you bend to stroke the dingo's coat—more like fur, like fire—I perceive you, not in a different light, but through a new glimpse of your own making, yearning for a simpler life directed by this animal's patient demeanour: how you might clip a chain to his smart new collar and walk along the seafront, chatting with friends, or sit a while with coffee and watch the changing waves without the struggle to render their movements in paint, without the clock pressing in on you—like argument, like rent—until you crumple... this animal that doesn't belong to you (or anyone), that burns with fierce anxieties and desires of its own.

*

I'm staring out to sea when the book is placed on the bench beside me: *Invisible Cities*, wrapped with a simple orange cord, tied in a bow, its plain white cover impressed to make a window with a view of a single pen-line seagull crossing the white sky. I hear its call and look again across Coogee beach where a crowd has gathered by the shore, before I untie the cord and find an old postcard between pages: a sepia photograph of a Giudecca restaurant, and now it's a rat I hear scurrying through foliage beside the canal, time falling away, so that when I look up again the crowd has gone.

Snails

Your mother picked them, one
by one from plants in your garden,
dropping them into a jar of salt.
Your friend marvelled as they died
and though you tried

to call a halt
your mother indulged your guest
and carried on,
friendship dissolving to disgust.

From *The Encyclopedia of Forgotten Things*

When he charged, head down—index fingers levelled like horns—
it was your instinct first to stand your ground and then, at the last
moment, to step aside, leaving your brother to thump into the
tree, but when your mother—over the years—would say 'poor
David', it was you who winced, with nowhere to turn.

*

Your father still refused to take out the trees—five eucalypts
screening the house, sole survivors among the white picket fences
and open lawns—while opposite, a huge red river gum towered
over the slope of scrub where every ball would bounce away,
lost... You liked that house—its modern brick and blue tiled roof—
for all its cramped simplicity, and won't forget the afternoon you
sat there after school, low sun fanning deep shadows through the
trees, knowing that time would never again be wholly yours.

*

And to find the swivelling street-level view online, revealing the
house now further dwarfed by those three eucalypt trees—the
only building still the same—was to feel your schoolbag still swing
from your shoulder, and to imagine the creak of the door, leading
to a welcoming cool... so that when, weeks later, you tried it again
and the house, the trees, the whole charmingly simple garden was
gone, you knew it was no gimmick but another cruel removal
of everything you'd had and with which, for one moment, you
had still been blessed.

'Road Closed'

was emphatic,
but the rusty sign
hung on an open gate,
allowing me to kid myself
and drive on through—
up the narrow sandy track
in an erratic

    sequence
    of hairpin bends
    towards the summit,
    and as I continued,
    with ever less option
    to reverse, I began to forget
    the warning, my lapsed

judgement eclipsed
by glimpses of magnificence
beyond—hills, folding
to a pale blue
infinity—
until the sudden, huge stone
fallen into the road.

    I felt the absurdity
    as I tried first to move it,
    then—back in the car, holding
    my nerve—to gauge the space
    between rock
    and scarp,
    all to within an inch

of my life.
And for what?—
the view from the top?
My sense of privilege
was equally a trespass
on the sublime;
I longed to remain

in the melancholy
of my private wilderness
with time
and empty sky my friends,
rather than once again
face the crumbling precipice
of my own folly.

Bonsai, Canberra

for Thali

As you led me through
to the bonsai collection,
the café's busy murmur
dwindled to a hush.
I had seen such trees
only in pictures,
always in full leaf,

> so the bud-
> ding branches took
> me by surprise.
> How absurd—
> failing to conceive
> of their real world
> seasons. They enthralled

with their tightly furled
pale green tips, as if
an artist had merely
touched their filigree
with the finest brush.
You tried to explain
the strictures,

> the wires,
> clipped roots—cruel
> as the binding of small
> girls' feet. We ordered
> coffee and sat side
> by side, so that we both
> could look

down across
the city, clear as a plan.
The lake reminded me
of the miniature garden I made
from a compact mirror,
and pebbles, bordered
with moss—

       all for a competition.
       Our time was nearly
       up, but I was loath
       to leave.
       You asked if I knew
       what I wanted. I replied
       with a tight smile.

King's Canyon

was a road too far, a fact
that held with what I'd planned—
tempting as it was to veer
recklessly off-course—aware
that what I lacked

was the right companion
with whom to share
the risk of the red land
turning to red river.

Trilobite

As I came to the ravine
and the path ran out,
there was a fossil at my feet
like a primitive sign
in the rock. As with Mr Knight

in *A Pair of Blue Eyes*, it
was my single sight
of anything that had ever been alive
and had had a body to save.

Temporary Resident

I wormed my way in
to a niche, nourished;
an interloper tolerated,
humoured, excused;
a compliant cell in the gut
of the body politic,
gorging on sunshine, even

        in the dark; quarantine
        endured in the proximity
        of bliss; my days numbered
        by a malignant algorithm
        I failed to decode
        in the complacent slide
        from snug

to smug
as I paced the limited
measure of my cell,
such locomotion
forming the symbiotic
drift of my demise.
It was worms that

        turned on me with
        visceral indifference:
        they burrowed to my core,
        hollowed
        me out
        until I was pure alien,
        my comfortable niche

a mortichnium—
the pre-fossilized dom-
ain of my crawl
from grace—my heart-
beat a real-time death-
march drummed
with my own blood...

        ... a stay of execution,
        and in the fractional
        moment before I was
        gone, I had a glimpse
        of happiness—no more
        than a brief intensity
        of disintegrating dust.

We slip from the back of the boat

into the ocean and tread water with our fins. It's a dress rehearsal,
in wet suits and snorkelling masks, the crew assessing our
competence in the open sea for when the humpbacks approach,
and we are doing ok, but really we are poor, poor creatures, ill-
equipped for our research, our survival, even our play, because
today—for the first time in nine months of the year—the visibility
in the water won't do and the crew are shaking their heads: we're
not safe; and all the while some forty whales are gathering around
us, their delicate grunts and soundings so precise they might even
sense our dismay.

THE ART OF NOISE

We are slowed down sound and light waves, a walking bundle of frequencies tuned into the cosmos.
—Albert Einstein

I'm an analog man in a digital world.
—Joe Walsh

Oysters

In the cavernous underground space by the Grand Central Oyster Bar, New York, you can whisper to your friend or lover on the far side, over the madding crowd.

That first year there, I was part of the passing rush—to be married, but not before a long-planned boys-own adventure across the US of A. Tim decided to be Billy—it had more of an outlaw ring. We had the cowboy boots straight out of *Coogan's Bluff*, but with a backpack New York was a frustration—I couldn't wait for Niagara's cool spray on my face, or the horizons of Montana. We hitched through Yellowstone and on to Monterey where we sat for hours with coffee, and watched otters diving and cracking open shells with sophisticated ease. And when I think of a time I'd call carefree it was wandering the hills of San Francisco, looking down across the glittering bay—Alcatraz the sullen jewel in the middle, making it real.

In New Orleans we drank in a Bourbon Street bar and woke up in Miami. Little wonder our money had run out as we came full circle, back to New York. Our Long Island hosts-to-be were out of town so we slept rough in the park. Home, and I couldn't get the boots off fast enough, but the plans for marriage wouldn't last.

When I next saw Billy, he looked all wrong. His new motorbike had taken him into a tree.

I went back to the Oyster Bar once, and was shown how it worked.

Can you hear me, Billy? Tracy Louise?

Sometimes it seems that the best of life just slips down the throat.

Vaudeville

Winchester Cathedral
You're bringin' me down,
You stood and you watched as
My baby left town...
The dance band tune
with its megaphone
vocal drifted out

      of my mother's kitchen,
      nineteen sixty-six—
      the Light Programme
      mere months away
      from its demise.
      Frank and Petula were
      quick to cover it,

keen, like those
who whistled along
to the daffiness
of the song,
to affix
the full blame
on anyone

      but themselves—they all
      needed that gal
      and the alarm call
      of *your bell.*
      And all the while
      you held firm—wilful
      in your deafness.

I had no *baby*. My mind
was on football.
Still, I was in thrall
to the peculiar earworm—
a concept and a word
as yet unknown.
When you took

       me under your wing,
       I took your side,
       aloof, singing your
       praises, but
       there came a day
       I too would disappear.
       You offered no rebuke.

i.m. Geoff Stephens, 1934-2020

WYSIWYG

I ignored the manual—
it wasn't even the right
one, and didn't de-
code the acronyms:
HPF; LFO; PWM—
my initials!
But I liked the feel

       of the calibrated
       knobs and sliders,
       and although
       the instrument had no
       sound of its own—
       no *preset*, no *patch*—
       I could create one

from scratch,
adjusting the controls
until the visible markers
were a match
for what I wanted
to hear:
What You See

       Is What You Get.
.   Some dials had charm—
       Depth, Resonance—
       but four were crucial:
       Attack, Decay, Sustain,
       Release—the envelope
       in which to wrap

the subtly modulated
amplitude
of filtered square
or sawtooth wave
and give it soul—
science
the engineer

        of sentiment, mood...
        of a layered narrative,
        something akin
        to poetry, even love
        and other terms
        for which
        there were no dials.

'Dear Mum'

for Claire

It's a short chain
of letters written home
from the front,
each verse with that
same opening refrain.
You wrote the lyric:
I had an instant tune

      like some cut-
      price Elton John.
      Except it was Beethoven
      that I riffed on,
      borrowing the Allegretto
      from number seven.
      It's a little different

from our usual
post-punk fare, but
it's stranger still
when news comes through
of the General Belgrano
torpedoed, as we play,
by a British submarine,

      2nd of May,
      nineteen eighty-two.
      Three hundred and
      twenty-three Argentine
      troops are drowned;
      my Falkland Island
      cousins are under siege.

Mick's drums gain
a forceful edge—
a pseudo-military beat—
and the audience
who had come
just for a good time—
to dance—

> are thrown,
> not knowing anymore
> what the music
> (or their presence)
> is actually *for*.
> We're a sombre band
> packing up the gear.

Sound Effects

Paul's letter to the Corinthians is the first of the antiphons, speaking to itself across the years for the three who have worn the same Irish lace, pitching charity (though today it's love) above mere sounding brass or a tinkling cymbal. Later, after the short walk home, I listen to my own speech come back to me in a foreign tongue, and two Best Men make their stereo jokes before Sicilian and English song do friendly battle in the huge, fire-lit tent at the top of the field. This is the future, you tell me when the wedding breakfast is done—these multicultural bonds and their vociferous delight—and the band gives way to an iPod pumping its eclectic playlist late into the night. It will be one or maybe two in the morning that a policeman comes to quibble but then, seeing the noise is purest joy, responds with an affirmative retreat.

*

You can see the music in how they move, as if underwater, in the silent drift of stained glass light, a single tribe with ears like an insect's compound eyes, through which a choice of wireless soundwaves is delivered to their brains, then their muscles, without respite, so that when any one of them makes it to the bar, she shouts, convinced you can't hear her VODKA AND TONIC!

*

The village hall film club has subtitles that give captions for every scripted noise [sigh] [chuckle] [roar of wind] [an aeroplane overhead]. Looking around I see the audience is mostly tolerant, even appreciative; our ears have grown larger by the years, to little effect, but here we can rely on the literary approximation onscreen—the text sometimes outsizing the actors' gestures or the significance of the sound.

*

A body of water / breaks on the shore, pulled / by the moon, knowing just when / it must swell to a crest and / dash itself again / in a rhythmic dissolution / that's equally a re-gathering, / driven by the wind / or lulled... / / Listen to each wave as it approaches, / hauling enough mass at least / to revise its ponderous surges / for your distraction, as you sit alone / with your thoughts, on the sand, / holding your knees to your chest.

*

Molten bronze pours into the channel between cope and core, until it fills the whole ghostly, silent space where the false bell once held sway, the design laboriously pictured with wax. It cools here in the sandpit for a week, before the mantle and the outer mould are raised on a pulley and the vast bell hoisted from the inner mould to be tuned on a lathe, the partial frequencies— hum, prime, tierce, quint, nominal—all brought into harmonious accord, with no going back once the metal has been ground and a single strike-note achieved, be it a summons, a toll, or part of a peal. But don't fool yourself that the pitch will be the same for you, for me, here, there, from one day to the next.

*

Only by its absence do you notice the slow pulled tick of the grandfather clock, and its hourly chime, like the daily freight train that rattled past your bedroom window, waking you with its silence that morning it didn't come, but you don't yet know how the absence will grow, when the clock, no longer just wound down, is sold, and the house sold too, a whole life gone, and something clamours to be there, with the colossal force of a waterfall implausibly frozen in the air.

*

For everyone not inside your head it's a seething irrelevance: the rush of white water over the horseshoe falls; the surf that pounds you to the ocean floor in a sandblasted panic; cicadas in full frenzy, beating your eardrums with their buckling timbals; the Fizzy boys revving in the street, adolescence smoothing to a manageable hum, like nostalgia; the comfort of an old valve wireless before the tinniest transistor radio replaces it with yet more excruciating off-beam hiss; white noise from a synth circa 1981; a thicket of snakes; the first feint crackle of fire, like water tipped onto gravel, or crumpled tin foil, while you wait for the inevitable whoomph; the persistent wasp that won't let you alone, zooming in your face all afternoon while the other guests doze or are peacefully lost in their books; the Formula 1 drone, lap after tedious lap; the aeroplane's engine that won't let you sleep, on a journey that won't end.

*

You begin to wonder if your poems are each set in a certain key: this one, for instance, in C# minor, as you lie with nothing but your darkest, restless thoughts, a moonbeam drifting in through the roof-light on what was always her side of the bed, needling your sleep with a relentless, mournful, broken chord. The haunting is still present when you wake, your fingers slowly rippling on the pillow beside your face.

*

Listening back over his recordings, he could just make out a blackbird joining in, and was pleased—not just with the unexpected act of community, but the genuine harmony produced, and as he listened to his various attempts at the new song in different keys, he was astonished to hear how the blackbird re-pitched its counter melody to the guitar, and he abandoned the song, staring out of the window in search of his casual accomplice, who'd moved on.

*

You feel your way across the bedroom in the dark, your memory gauging the distance between one piece of furniture and the next, to the door, the stairs, and you think of Mr Lecky, survivor of that unnamed catastrophe, prowling the department store in which he is trapped. It's the script they would return to, Peckinpah and Silke, whenever there was time to kill, falling into their old routine ('he'd get the meats, I'd get the peanut butter and bread, we'd fight over the ice cream'), facing their own demons, digging deeper at the story, digging so deep there was no way out, making *Castaway* their reality. And every sound comes to haunt you: a squirrel scratching at the moss on the roof, the creak of a shrinking pipe, the bark of a dog long dead, and the clock, the clock that tells you this isn't a dream, that you won't wake up.

*

Her letter is unopened in his green jacket pocket as Leo is hurried on his way by your fugue—across a field, a fateful summer, England, the past, or is it the future—through the heat, a new century, a thirteenth birthday (unlucky for some), and as he pauses by the tree we fear the worst, for all the beauty of your nouveau baroque. The music is the go-between for the boy you once were and the man who reads that counterpointed, breathless, 'darling darling darling' on the page.

*

Opening the drawer, I find a jumble of old cassettes, some labelled, some not; some in the wrong hard plastic cases (some of them broken, or cracked)—Blondie masquerading as Verdi, *The Enigma Variations* as *Aladdin Sane*—and a blank one proving to be *By Jeeves!* An indistinct recording in an Eastern European accent (from a lecture? the radio?) about melting ice-caps is a mystery. Then there's music I wrote myself, and my own voice reading poetry on the BBC. It's a catalogue of surprises, the level of startlement destined to fall—until I stumble on the pencilled date, 31st October, 1981, and as I slip the forgotten tape into the deck and press play, I hear not only a famous toccata, but a pivotal six minutes of my life: the breathy detail of that autumnal afternoon; a ritual concluded; everyone making their way from the church to where the music stops.

White Noise

for Clare

In winter
people stand here
in front of a massive frieze,
the Gullfoss waterfall
at a standstill.
Today, the water
plunges and drives

       through its familiar
       self-made channel,
       forming the backdrop
       as I line up
       the last photo I will
       ever take of you.
       The sounding cataract

will haunt me
like a passion. You smile,
as people always do,
with automatic ease;
trickier by far
to catch Geysir
blasting into the air.

       Later, it's Jökulsárlón,
       the glacier lagoon,
       then Þingvellir—
       the place two
       continents meet,
       or rather separate,
       a visible rift of tect-

onic plates, growing
by the year.
We return
for Happy Hour—
the iced fire
at six—little knowing
that this is as happy

as our lives
together will permit
before the awful fact—
in all its tumultuous din—
that I need to be
somewhere else
crashes in.

Rhyme

I rhyme / to see myself, to set the darkness echoing.
    —Seamus Heaney

I've been described as someone who would rhyme 'cat' with 'dog'.
    —Paul Muldoon

They slept in the same basket in front of the fire, the old black lab and the older white cat—deaf from birth, the green of his eyes dispersed into one yellow and one blue—in the aftermath of their dangerous play, the dog's jaw almost encircling the cat's whole head: and here are you and I, aligned, so that back rhymes with chest, and my hand (wrapped around you) with your breast.

*

Brother and sister would play in the deep snow covering their garden, inventing their own rhymes; a Bear of very little brain sometimes joined them in their innocent song, adding the occasional *tiddely pom*, and once—as his footprints came full circle—it seemed that he was tracking something, maybe a Woozle, and when Piglet arrived, they circled again, and imagined the Woozle had been joined by a Wizzle, and so it went on...

*

Jack Torrance is not far behind him as he runs, terrified, into the maze, an eerie blue light shining through the snow... he changes track, this way and that; his footprints are a give-away and yet—as if with experience beyond his years—he knows to make use of them: stopping, then moving backwards, retracing his own steps as perfectly as he can, one agonisingly slow stride at a time; he has no idea why he's become an abhorrence to his father, he just knows that each repeated impression in the snow must match... finally he leaps clear and carefully brushes over his escape—or so he hopes, hiding behind the hedge as the maniacal wind plays on, and his father limps past, clutching the axe...

Nothing rhymed with orange, he'd been told ('job done then' he joked while carrying on with his fruitless task). But he liked a challenge, and would forage through the cupboards, pausing over a box of Scots porridge oats, and putting aside a solitary lozenge for some other occasion. For lunch he settled on a range of cheeses, with carrot soup rather splendidly served in a rare silver porringer. It was late in the day that he turned his mind to funghi, algae, mosses and ferns, and their various sporangia, reckoning that the sac of a single sporange (as he legitimately clipped it) might yield the jackpot of a thousand spores.

*

Now and then I glimpse a foreshadowing: my father on ciné film, helping me down from the playground roundabout and suddenly clutching his knee, some thirty years before I'd feel the same sharp twinge as I twist, scything grass in the field, as if pain were passing from one body to another, one generation to the next; or psoriasis, starting as a single patch of rough red skin, fired by stress to spread its cruel cartography on beauty's blank page; and the moment by the Reflecting Pool, at the steps to the Memorial you so wanted to see, when, breathless, you chose to stop short.

*

Peckinpah Mountain looms three thousand feet above Peckinpah Creek and Peckinpah Meadow where the lumber mill used to be; we're driving the old timber trail—Peckinpah Road, north of North Fork—in a convoy, each landmark triggering a song; a bottle goes around as we pass Whisky Falls towards Shuteye Ridge... it's getting dark, *too dark to see*, and it all goes quiet in our truck as the rhymes give way to a single, sombre refrain we share silently in our heads *just like so many times before... knock knock knocking on heaven's door, knock knock knocking on heaven's door...*

'Assuming Equilibrium'

Amy has had enough
of her husband
retreating to his study
and equations.
She'll thumb
a piece of chewing gum
on his blackboard

> and change a plus
> to a minus
> when he's not looking.
> But David Sumner
> won't let his wife screw
> with the math. You watch
> her in bed—

while he attempts to wind
the clock—working
on the *Straw Dogs* score.
The endless exertions
of *The Wild Bunch*
almost cost you
your own marriage.

> This time you know
> it must be simpler,
> faster; the faux
> Stravinsky will prove
> a good match.
> And now you're ready
> for *The Getaway*—McQueen

and McGraw
in the dream–team heist,
the real life
couple who on screen
are falling apart.
It's love
that slaps her hard

> across the face.
> You view it on repeat
> until you find the right
> ambience,
> the perfect balance:
> *like a man in a green suit*
> *walking in a forest.*

i.m. Jerry Fielding, 1922-1980

Desert Island Discs

For eighty years
the music washes over us—
By the Sleepy Lagoon—
echoing with gulls.
The formula is sublime:
you're a castaway, somewhere
between paradise

      and hell, by virtue
      of your celebrity status.
      Your survival kit:
      eight chosen musical tracks;
      the complete works
      of Shakespeare;
      the Bible (or preferred

alternative text); one
further book; plus
a luxury item. It's a scheme
that never fails:
Hitchcock can look forward
to his forthcoming *Psycho*;
Brian Rix reappears

      as if through the doors
      of a bedroom farce;
      churlish to name
      the guest who chose nothing
      but her own fabulous
      recordings, clearly at ease
      with her solitary self.

And as we listen, we all
long to have a go—
lining up those favourites
that tell the essential
story of our lives.
You already have it off pat,
and you'll either refuse

      the Bible, or tear out
      the pages for lighting
      fires. But the (inanimate)
      luxury item gives
      you sleepless nights:
      you're taking this
      too seriously by half.

Hungarian Rhapsody

Franz Liszt hurries in a post-chaise towards his next triumph: Caroline de Saint-Criq; Bettina von Arnim; Charlotte von Hagn; Marie Duplessis; Marie Pleyel; Lola Montez; Olga Janina; Pauline Viardot-Garcia; Emilie Merian-Genast; Caroline Unger-Sabatier; Eveline Hańska; Agnes Street Klindworth; Sofie Menter; Baroness Olga von Meyendorff; George Sand; Princesses Carolyne von Sayn-Wittgenstein and Cristina Trivulzio di Belgiojoso; and the countless countesses, Maria von Mouchanoff, Adèle Laprunarède, Rosalie Sauerma, Marie Cathérine Sophie d'Agoult—just listen to those fingers play!

THE ROMANTICS

Deep inside us all there is something that speaks to us and drives us, almost unconsciously, and that may emerge at times sounding as poetry or music.
—Johannes Brahms

Do yourself a favor and go find the originals.
—Guns 'n Roses

Ludwig van Beethoven

Sinfonia Eroica (1803)

When you hear that Bonaparte has appointed himself Emperor,
you lose your rag, crossing out the dedication with such fury you
scuff a hole in the page   before
tearing it up,   for good measure. Then
you get ahead of yourself too, at bar 394, the horn announcing the
return of the main theme, two bars early, clashing with the strings.
Haydn is speechless, head in hands; even Berlioz thinks you've lost
it, ffs, but you're deaf to the critique. Later, overwhelmed by a
torrent of silence, you beat the keyboard senseless, so that listeners
struggle to hear any order in the jangling cacophony. Slowly,
over the course of the next two hundred years, our hearing comes
back. *I'd give this piece four stars. Stumbled on the YouTube film,
thinking it said Erotica, but hey—not bad!*

Eroica, dir. Cellan Jones, 2003

Hector Berlioz

Symphonie Fantastique: Épisode de la vie d'un artiste ... en cinq parties (1830)

He's in the theatre that night, as Hamlet lifts poor Yorick's skull, travelling through time. It could be David Tennant, holding Tchaikovsky's remains like a glass of water to the light; it could be anyone; it doesn't matter; Hector only has eyes for Harriet Smithson as Ophelia, instantly obsessed. When she fails to reply to his letters, he assembles a team of crack musicians, clad in black. They play by heart, the artist's unrequited passion—his delirium—seared into their brains. And so it erupts, symphony as story; the woman who ignores him the *idée fixe* within the soundtrack of his life.

And we're with him all the way—the delusional lord of the dance—as he drags us down, deeper and down ... There's a moment of calm, a day when the *ranz des vaches* is calling to me across an alpine meadow from the past, with dark questions that I can't answer.

The music grows feverish, murderous in its dreams. It's a trip to hell. *Long aerial tracking shot of a yellow beetle travelling through the mountains to the Overlook Hotel.*

And now the musicians don white paper masks like skeletal, antlered beasts from a wild, wild wood; eyes wide shut. Red light falls like a curtain of blood on their black sabbath.

Reader, he married her!

The Shining, dir. Kubrick, 1980

Aurora Orchestra plays Berlioz's Symphonie Fantastique—by heart, Aurora Orchestra, YouTube 2019

Niccolò Paganini

Moto Perpetuo (1835)

Gone are the ephemeral lovers' sighs of your Duetto Amoroso, those gasping phrases that tugged at the heartstrings eschewed in favour of machine-gun 16ths: 187 measures of the same, frenzied as Pike Bishop at the Battle of Bloody Porch, the circular breathing of your Marfan fingers defying the laws of physics—and time—and by the law of averages it's never stopped... there's no escape ... someone, somewhere in the world is always playing it: 'Il faut risquer', as every fiddle player knows, battling their demons—I'll bet a fiddle of gold against your soul, I think I'm better than you—go on, try it: cut the cop-out cadential chords at 188 and 189 and put it on repeat; keep the software updated; keep the electricity bill paid, the devil at bay, your bid for the future a mash-up of the past

Hellraiser Went Down to Georgia, Motörhead & Primus, RaveDJ, 2019

Frédéric Chopin

Prelude, Op. 28, No. 15 ('Raindrop') (1839)

I walk past the end of the white-rosed garden into the field, and beyond, over Round Top Hill, painted with poppies, into the bluebell wood. The sun filters through, and then it's gone, there's a chill in the air and I don't want to be here anymore. The walk back home takes twice as long, unless it's quicker—I can't tell. I sit at the Broadwood piano, unable to play. For every imaginary raindrop there's a spot of human blood, coughed onto ivory. Behind my eyes, the bluebell haze is the colour of tuberculosis. It was Bach who kept you company, along with your lover, as the weather failed you in Majorca; Jagger, in white frock coat who turned to Shelley in Hyde Park, Brian Jones dead in his swimming pool. *Peace, peace! he is not dead, he does not sleep / He has awakened from the dream of life…* …My fingers begin to move. I manage a little Bach, a little Chopin. A cloud of white butterflies is released, but the crowd doesn't see the thousands that don't make it out of the cardboard boxes.

Bright Star, dir. Campion, 2009

Clara Schumann

Konzertsatz (1847, unfinished)

Your father names you for the clarity of his purpose, but you have your own; it just won't come as words. Eleven years old and you're rewriting the future, playing from memory, switching the audience on to Bach; somewhere, Glenn Gould is listening in. Franz Lang Lang Liszt can toss his head back like a diva—you don't want to know: *the personality of the musician should be suppressed*. But not the woman, oh no, though you'll find yourself the only one on the faculty of the Frankfurt Konservatorium. You release your husband's *Papillons*, even while your own masterpiece waits in the wings. Eight children, and still you're performing. You walk through the battle zone of Dresden to retrieve the three left behind. The Opera House is burnt to the ground, but there's worse to come; Billy Pilgrim—*unstuck in time*—has already told us, accompanied by Gould, taking us back to Bach yet again, though so little it won't fill an album. Four of your children die and you gather their offspring to your own brood. *So it goes.* And still your Konzertsatz waits for the words it deserves: *If the first full concerto is pedestrian, this fragment inspires that art can be made in those spare moments when the hands are already exhausted from their breadwinning ways.*

Slaughterhouse-Five, dir. Hill, 1972

For JW

Modest Mussorgsky

Pictures at an Exhibition—A Remembrance of Viktor Hartmann
(1874)

Stunned by the death of your friend, you knock it out in three weeks, walking through his paintings and onward—into the catacombs, with the dead in a dead language, but your promenade reappears, and you enter the heroic gate of peerless virtuosity. Ravel has a good stab at it, his remake in colour. Emerson Lake and Palmer crank it up to the max, with the Newcastle City Organ and a modular Moog. We blare it out from our common room window, driving the old masters mad. The promenade goes on. The years assemble paintings into galleries of our own. Every summer we stack the fridge with beers and it's 'Welcome back my friends, to the show that never ends.' The promenade goes on. But Emo begins to suffer from 'writer's cramp' in his right hand; his GX-1 is sold to Hans Zimmer. I break our run of summers, living abroad. When I'm finally home, I open a crate of pictures to find a mess of broken glass, The Queen of the Seas within an inch of her life. Hartmann's own pictures are mostly lost, though Baba Yaga's hut—depicted as a clock—still stands on its chicken feet, the witch of the east careening through your scherzo with her pestle and mortar, grinding our future to dust. Emo's quick-draw hand is painfully slow as he raises a gun to his head in Santa Monica. The promenade is at an end. Our last reunion is in hospital. I write the eulogy, make suggestions for the music. In a few weeks, lockdown.

The Wizard of Oz, dir. Fleming, 1939

i.m. KNE, 1944–2016; MTND, 1958–2020

Richard Wagner

Götterdämmerung (1876)

I place daffodils in the violin-shaped vase that is really a bottle,
emptied of some duty-free liqueur from the long weekend when
you became *the loveliest girl in Vienna*. It was a treat, not a trick, to
take you away from your comfortable Friday night routine. The
city knew we had something to celebrate: the bars were strung
with cobwebs, a pumpkin on every table; the same story for each
of our thirty-five years; three more, since then, when it's been
merely Halloween. That day, Mozart's statue was starkly white
against autumn leaves. We missed Klimt's kiss in the Belvedere—a
long weekend is only so long, though the whole Ring cycle was
written to fit. We caught the last five hours—*Twilight*—with
champagne between acts. The words, in translation, scrolled past
on miniature seatback screens while the music thundered. But
twilight, it strikes me now, is not easily understood: it may seem
to last forever, but it's little more than the fleeting brush of day
against night.

Inspector Morse, 'Twilight of the Gods', dir. Wise, 1993

i.m. CEMM, 1959–2017

Arthur Sullivan

'The Lost Chord' (1877)

I sit by my father's bed, watching him die—though I don't yet
know it. He won't move again, now, though he was longing for
a view of the sea—to get away from these claustrophobic woods
he used to love. The woods, perhaps, are partly the problem: his
imaginings, darker. Today it's the memory that closes in on me,
thinking how my mother already knew that view of the sea would
be hers alone. Gilbert and Sullivan first brought them together:
impossible to mention one without the other. But I think of
Sullivan, by his dying brother's bedside, finding a poetic chord
elsewhere: *It quieted pain and sorrow, like love overcoming strife; it
seemed the harmonious echo from our discordant life.*

Topsy Turvy, dir. Leigh, 2000

i.m. PCEM, 1911–1976; BEM, 1921–1980

Bedřich Smetana

String Quartet No. 1, 'From My Life' (1878)

Antonín Dvořák played viola at the private premiere, in Prague, but you're more likely to have seen Victoria Miskolczy entertaining Robert Redford and his gang. The encryption is unchanged: the same four instruments in intimate debate; the same closed circle of conversation... until that moment the circuit breaks, the code is cracked, a long, sustained, harmonic eeeeeeeeeeeeeeeeeee drilling the air straight from the composer's head; his tinnitus—itself the effect of time—unleashed, drilling your own eardrums, the *me* (of *time*), that was once an inaudible, background hum, now morphing to a mundening drone that drives you out of your mind.

Sneakers, dir. Robinson, 1992

Charles–Marie Widor

Toccata, from Symphony for Organ No. 5 (1879)

It plays as the boys spill out of chapel, dreaming of revolt:
motorbikes, leathers, girls, (and yes) guns. Our own small act of
rebellion was simply to slow it right down — into a grungy
calypso with lilting bass, top line overlaid on a
languorous synth, everyone on their feet in the
sweltering basement of the Olde Worlde Club... We
pulled out all the stops, while others pulled bottles
of Black Bush from behind the unmanned bar...
And yeah, we were trashed after those gigs, but
the music was somehow unscathed, the shiny toccata
emerging a year later, back up to speed, as you and I walked
down the aisle, some of the same faces beaming in the crowd, the
music itself now punching the air with a congregated *Yes!*

If, dir. Anderson, 1968

For TE, MG, CO

Camille Saint-Saëns

'Kangaroos' from *The Carnival of the Animals* (1886)

It's four hands at play, on two pianos—the reason the kangaroos are at once quietly grazing and bouncing off, a finger-flick levering the triads that gain velocity up the keyboard, before falling away. So purely joyous, so frivolous, you feared for your reputation—*On no account publish this until after my death*—failing to envision your more serious symphony with Farmer Hogget singing to a pig. The modern Olympics kick off, but it's a century later that inflatable kangaroos storm the stage as the Sydney games are announced.

[Splice in verses by Ogden Nash, read by Roger Moore.]

It's a reliable party piece, a mere minute long, but in the 2020 Namadji remix, it's not so much fun; no grace notes to help the roos outpace the blazing grass. The sound, for days—for weeks, months—is the roar of air, sucked into hell. The concert stage is a wasteland of blackened bones.

If I had words to make a day for you, I'd sing you a morning golden and new. I would make this day last for all time; give you a night deep in moonshine.

Babe, dir. Noonan, 1995

For TBW

Claude Debussy

Claire de Lune (1890, rev. 1905)

Fifteen years for the moonlight to be polished. In the water,
a waxing reflection of his fame. Verlaine's songbird, forlorn,
becomes a nightingale, *magic abroad in the air*... The ruptured
tendon in my left hand leaves the bass notes adrift, and the image
blurs—like my tearful vision, *an echo far away*. The song is stolen
from a story. *I may be right, I may be wrong*. Enraptured. Or forlorn.
Les grands jets d'eau play against the Bellagio Hotel. Water, water,
every where, as he shifts from his impressionist *Nocturnes* to *La
Mer*. Now my arms span the keyboard, the vast harmonic spread
of a single chord hauling *La cathedrale engloutie* into the light—the
sound so transparent you can hear the bells—even as William
Walker, the Winchester Diver, does the same with hammer
and pick. You stood at the west end of the nave the night I was
there in the choir, processing past the candle-lit tree, my surplice
brushing against your skin. Beauty. Beauty is sadness, sadness ...
The world goes under. *The streets of town were paved with stars...*
I met you after work outside your office in Berkeley Square. *Our
homeward step was just as light as the tap-dancing feet of Astaire.*

Ocean's Eleven, dir. Soderbergh, 2002

Engelbert Humperdink

Hänsel und Gretel (1892)

You follow a breadcrumb trail through the woods, thinking how the son must be cast as a mezzo-soprano. You're a little late to give Siegfried his lesson; by the time you're there, it's not so much Siegfried as a silvered Rick Wakeman rising from Wagner's operating table, grabbing a stein of beer, belching, and pissing on the fire. ('Who's going to follow *him?*' laughs Daltrey-as-Lizst.) The trail doubles back to your more famous faux namesake, crooning his hit cover on a 45-year rollercoaster to Eurovision doom. Suddenly the weather is closing in: the woods are darkening, even as quick snowflakes obliterate the crumbs. Soon the lines are down, the roads all closed. The witch locks up. Wagner's great-great-grandson sits alone in his snowbound studio, giving up on us and writing the TV soundtrack himself. Somewhere, in development, is the Hansel module with *user-customised rules independent from the menu system*, logic switches adding links to the crumbs. Richard Strauss will conduct, Ringo Starr put in a cameo as the Pope. Arnold George Dorsey, post-tuberculosis, keeps 'Penny Lane' off the number one spot, and as war breaks out they won't appoint a German to the Sydney Conservatorium—it's enough to give anyone the hump. Adrian Wagner rubs the Sandman's grit from his eyes and adjusts the mix as a super-bronzed Theseus belts out to Ariadne: *Please release me, let me go... Release me and let me love again.*

Lisztomania, dir. Russell, 1975

i.m. AW, 1952-2018

Antonín Dvořák

Symphony No. 9, 'From the New World' (1893)

The musicassette cover shows me—or someone—crouching above the Grand Canyon, from the days I was in love with America. Today, that's not possible. But as the music plays, I'm tugged back; it's irresistible. A new century is ushered in, full of longing for things left behind. You leave your burrow, blinking into the blinding light.

It was one of these mysterious fairy calls from out the void that suddenly reached Mole in the darkness, making him tingle through and through with its very familiar appeal, even while as yet he could not remember what it was. He stopped dead in his tracks, his nose searching hither and thither in its efforts to recapture the fine filament, the telegraphic current, that had so strongly moved him. A moment, and he had caught it again; and with it this time came recollection in fullest flood.

A boy pushes his bike up the slope of a Cotswold village, sepia toned. The Ashington Colliery Brass Band is at his side, telling us the Old World is still here, though it's not what it used to be. *Hovis*. The day I'm unwell, my father does my paper round, and I never pay him back.

Boy on the Bike, dir. Scott, 1973

Richard Strauss

Also Sprach Zarathustra (1896)

As the monolithic open chord dawns yet again, who can rid their mind of Kubrick's apes, picking a thighbone from the ground and thinking it into a weapon, drumming the skeletal remains and picturing how a fully-fleshed tapir might likewise be ruthlessly drummed into the dust. It's a small step, but a giant leap, to beat that same rhythm on a fellow ape, thus becoming man. The thighbone is hurled in slow motion into the air—and onward, into the vast, *eternal recurrence of the same*, the bone a baton, passed to Peckinpah reading Robert Ardrey, who hands it, an iron poker, to Dustin Hoffman as David Sumner, timid mathematician, beating an intruder's head to a pulp. It's a twilight zone of soft-spoken, angry young men—so many one-eyed jacks—but it's the Valkyries who usher in the ultimate carnage, their shrill Wagnerian battle cry pumped out from speakers slung beneath the choppers storming in off the coast, machine guns adding their diegetic rattle as we journey further still into the heart of darkness. Upstream is the slobbery, corrupted übermensch, Colonel Kurtz—the same Brando who cut first Sam, then Stanley from his obsessive pet project, superstardom gone to his straw-filled head—himself now hacked to death, with an innocent buffalo cleavered into pieces live onscreen as ritual accompaniment. It's hard to watch, hard to listen—to a fanfare for the whimpering end of the world.

One-Eyed Jacks, dir. Brando, 1961

2001: A Space Odyssey, dir. Kubrick, 1968

Straw Dogs, dir. Peckinpah, 1971

Apocalypse Now, dir. Coppola, 1979

Edward Elgar

Variations on an Original Theme, 'Enigma' (1899)

All I wish is, that it may be a lesson to the world, 'to let people tell their stories their own way.' —Laurence Sterne

Tell me, Nigel, were you a bit Brahms and Liszt the time you set off fireworks on Elgar's grave, with Yehudi? Did you think you'd cracked the coded secret buried there? Or were you fashioning some controversial portraits of your own? Maybe not portraits, just those small character details that intrigue: your John Lennon shades, the brief beard, the blue and black kaftan; a boy on a white pony, later on a bike, always under an open sky. Let the boy ride free, the camera freely following ... The full theme never appears, like a principal character remaining offstage; your alcoholic father in Australia. Your *IN-GER-LAND* chant reverberates around the Malvern Hills as yet another rocket goes up. Were you channelling the dead man's notorious japes? He's still turning in his grave, his greatest tune hijacked by words not his, used as accompaniment to war and the waving of every Union Jack. He'd have been happier stony broke: Alice drawing staves, no money for ruled paper; going without fires for a year—Alice, his lifelong love with whom he buried his honours. But what of the other Alice, the Windflower of the concerto? *Aqui está encerrada el alma de* ..... Alice—or maybe Helen; the list goes on. The biggest enigma is what 'Nimrod' is doing at the end of *Australia*. O Baz, what were you *thinking*? And yet, you did it right (Laurence Sterne would be proud), even while getting it so wrong.

Elgar, dir. Russell, 1962

Australia, dir. Luhrmann, 2008

Maurice Ravel

Pavane pour une infante défunte (1899)

As if. A Spanish Princess from another age comes to life.
Velázquez stares out from his own canvas; his brushstrokes turn to
swirling brocade. Critics register a complaint when you perform
it yourself, 'unutterably slow', but when others are slower still
you've a deadpan quip to hand: It's not a *dead pavane*. The Princess
continues her stately steps like an automaton. Beautiful plumage.
Fast forward to the 30s and it's slower still, with lyrics almost
warbling to a halt like a failing reel-to-reel.   *Dream   and   watch
the   shadows   come   and   go,   the   lamp   is   low.* It's
Gaspard de la nuit who escorts the Princess back into the painterly
shadows. Now change the tape to something more upbeat. Tell
Cassandra to get her skates on.

10, dir. Edwards, 1979

For CA

Jean Sibelius

Finlandia (1899–1900)

A stone's throw from the beach. Paavo Berglund pulls the Bournemouth Symphony Orchestra through the beat. They're used to it, now, his wayward precision, and you yourself approve: the notes should *swim in the gravy*. In the interval I buy friends underage drinks from the Winter Gardens bar. Paavo's son Pokku and I play violin at school, and on a trip to Germany he blags us seats at the Berlin Philharmonic. At Checkpoint Charlie we have to change currency, then can't find anything to buy. When I return, the wall is gone, rewritten by Roger Waters. The Sony Centre towers over Potsdamer Platz. I can't take it in. I think of your *Finlandia* fail-better rewrites: re-titling, disguising the anti-Russian protest at its core; stripping it back for solo piano; giving it words—and letting others do the same, your music gifted both to stir and still the soul—all the while drinking your way into reclusive decline. 'The Silence of Järvenpää'. I think of the terror—of knowing your best work is behind you—as I sit at the keyboard and stare. *Turn your musical vision into compelling scores for the stage or screen with Sibelius software*. I google Pokku and find he owns a Bordeaux winery. He's written a book: *Wine of the Mind*. Everywhere online there's news of the pandemic. The heatwave soars, and Bournemouth beach is shingled with lager cans, heaving with bodies. Drink again. Drink harder. The sea is like soup.

Die Hard 2, dir. Harlin, 1992

i.m. PB, 1929–2012

For PH

Sergei Rachmaninoff

Piano Concerto No. 2 (1900-1)

What to do, as the century rolls over and Romanticism's dubbed old hat? You pull it tighter over your ears. Soon will come the charge that such sentiment is treacherous tosh. Hey ho. Another revolution and it's Valentine's Day in the Royal Station Hotel, Carnforth. Opposite is the Station Heritage Centre, where we enjoy a light lunch in the Brief Encounter Refreshment Room. *There's something in my eye.* It's a fleck of the past, as I sit with my father in front of the TV. Why would this possibly work in Winchester, with Richard Burton and Sophia Loren? My father switches it off. Bereft of inspiration, you drive around Beverly Hills in your swanky Ford Exile. *Couples particularly like the location—they rated it 8.8 for a two-person trip. We speak your language!*

Brief Encounter, dir. Lean, 1945

Alma Mahler Gropius Werfel

'Einsamer Gang' (2018 [1899])

A secessionist kiss from Gustav Klimt, and so it begins—a lonely walk through a succession of loves, marriages and affairs, barefoot in the rain. At each new encounter she leans in, seductively close, being deaf in one ear from a childhood illness. We all fall for it. She longs to write an opera, even as Kokoschka longs to parade her on his arm at the Teatro La Fenice—goes further, commissioning a full-sized doll in her image, careful that every curve should be perfectly modelled to the memory of his touch. His obsession lingers in our darkest routines. The footfalls we hear behind us mark the path that we follow—along the Fondamenta Contarini to the Casa Mahler, now a hotel—through the gate into her garden; a private paradise, refuge from the world. Later, on the Lido, it's her husband's Adagietto that we hear as Visconti persuades us that Aschenbach—longing for a beautiful boy—was a composer, not a writer, but the music is longing for no-one but her, whoever she may be: saint, sinner, or just another misunderstood young girl, a Bernadette. Did the puppet-maker misconstrue, upholstering her lower body with *feathers*? Did Kokoschka, artist, think that an artwork—more than a mere mortal—cannot be rejected, or ignored? Aschenbach's cholera overshadows the disease to which Alma's daughter Manon succumbs, her infantile paralysis the driving force of a sublime concerto 'to the memory of an angel'. 'Lähmungsakkord' is scrawled in the score—and from afar, a Carinthian folksong sounds like lost innocence. Is every affliction blessed by art? Or is it a fate worse than polio, death, to be a *Randfigur*—a muse to the more famous? They were all over her, like flies. *Es ist genug... lös auf das Band, das allgemählich reißt.* As the sun on the Lido begins to fade, I watch you dive and disappear for so long I begin to panic, thinking the current has dragged you under, away... ... but then you surface, and shake back the water from your hair in a glittering arc. The sparkle seems to hang in the air. Heads turn, as if witnessing a vision.

The Song of Bernadette, dir. King, 1943 (from the novel by Franz Werfel)

Death in Venice, dir. Visconti, 1971

For FED

Sir William Harris

'Bring Us O Lord God' (1959)

Barely thirteen, I don't think twice about having tea with a cathedral organist of the 19th century. I do think there was toast, as I can hear the whispering scrunch scrunch of a knife across the surface. All too soon it's time to go. Your protégé—our choirmaster—drives us back to school. All too soon it's a hearse at the door, first yours, then his; your music the soundtrack; words by John Donne. We mill around in the aisle, afterwards, wondering what to say. We're as lost as Henry Kissinger, Luciano Pavarotti and Sir Elton John—assembling as your prelude ends. Doc H—do they remember you, the sisters in black, from their madrigal practice at Windsor during the war? A full century has passed since you took your place at the organ in St David's, Wales. Words by John Donne; words by Bernie Taupin, David Dimbleby; words of my own, left in the village church pew as I too prepare to play the organ for an English rose. 'And so it ends, with the hearse heading north, under the Scratchwood motorway service station', *to enter into that gate... where there shall be no darkness nor dazzling, but one equal light; no noise nor silence, but one equal music; no fears nor hopes, but one equal possession; no ends nor beginnings, but one equal eternity...*

The Funeral of Princess Diana, BBC, 1997

i.m. CCMcW, 1934–2007

REPRISE

These memories, which are my life—for we possess nothing certainly
except the past—were always with me. Like the pigeons of St Mark's,
they were everywhere, under my feet, singly, in pairs, in little honey-voiced
congregations.
—Evelyn Waugh, *Brideshead Revisited*

We all dream of being a child again, even the worst of us.
—from *The Wild Bunch*

I bring down

all the old clutter, the dead
weight from the loft.
One old grey suitcase
bears my grandfather's initials.
Crammed inside

are old stuffed toys
and there, with those dimples,
your favourite doll. As I lift
her, she opens her eyes.

The Yellow Room

for Anouska

For you, your childhood bedroom would always be the yellow room, even as the walls changed colour over the years, and you moved out—first to the larger room along the corridor, then to university and finally abroad, and into marriage, your initials changing to span the whole alphabet. I repaint it yet again, a dusky blue, and bring back in, from the shed, the dolls' house I modelled on the home in which it sits once more like a nested matryoshka, for your children to explore. I clean off the cobwebs, open the roof and reveal the miniature rooms unchanged for a quarter century, with original wallpaper, carpets, memories, a little gramophone player: the yellow room still yellow; your name still matching mine.

My grandson

wanders around the house
as if it's unknown terrain
but he remembers every detail
and is bewildered by what's gone.
Where's Mimi, he says,

confronted with the age-old trial
of curiosity; the difficult equation
between memory and loss
that we struggle to explain.

Not So Fast

It was a family joke—
that I could run
before I learned to walk.
Then came the fierce
and frequent admonition
in the school corridor,
though it took

      a corner collision
      and spectacular black
      eye to tell me off best.
      Later, my speed
      brought applause
      and was the reason
      I'd be chosen

for a team.
But it was all raw
energy, lacking technique.
One day, someone
took the time
to show me the problem:
how my knees splayed

      outward as I made
      my manic dash for the line.
      I was told to slow down,
      to concentrate on
      keeping them
      aligned, to work
      at it week

after tortuous
week—all in the interest
of being faster still.
And though youth
and patience are rarely
friends, I kept faith
with the plan.

These days
it comes naturally,
knees prepared
for the occasional
twinge
completing each hard
lap of the village.

Fauré Requiem

After my nervous treble
solo, there's an interminable
wait for the cathedral voice trial
result; half a century till
the piece goes on hold

yet again—the village hall
closed for the year,
the Bulmer Choir
cancelled.

Memory Palace

for Mattia

Mine is a simple glass
shelf of miniature turtles
named from my travels.
The roll call is easy, but then
your small hands lift them

and give each one
a totally different name
from some imaginative place
beyond my ken.

Slowly, Quietly

The giant tortoises return
from their glamorous
Venetian sojourn
to where they belong, out-
numbering the people
of the islands, each
given copious greetings

> and a prominent spot
> within the Aéroport
> de la Pointe Larue.
> They have acquired
> the celebrity status
> of their creators,
> admired

for having taken
their unfashionable
theme—of longevity,
serenity, patience, hope—
into the cut-throat
global arena of fine art
and lived to tell

> the tale.
> The jazz tortoise
> continues to improvise—
> with violin, sax,
> and a circular keyboard
> around the fluted rim
> of his shell.

The one with wings
has gained credibility
as a frequent flyer;
another is still in manacles;
it's a message
that mustn't disappear.
But where are the critics,

> the crowds? What
> next for any local hero?
> Their life now predictable,
> they're less like radicals,
> more like washed-up
> superstars needing a fix
> of cocaine; a trifle glum.

The Very Same

for Patrick, and Gill

The day you marry,
in the cathedral,
I'm too young to take in
the full adventure—
or the risk. Instead, I feel
a bewildering worry
that it's all

        beyond my reach... but
        there was champagne,
        caviar, things
        I didn't really appreciate
        but could brag about,
        as if weddings
        were there to get

the better of us;
strange and dubious
claims to fame.
The week you die
half a century
later, with dementia,
your wife, now

        widow
        whom I once called
        the most beautiful
        woman in the world—
        the very same—
        phones with the news.
        A pause.

Then: *Paul*—
how old are you?
The simple question
floors me, but I smile
and finally reply:
sixty-two—
at which it's her turn

        to be thrown,
        having in mind
        that boy of thirteen
        who ran like the wind
        —oh yes, but not
        so fast as to out–
        run time.

Brideshead Revisited

Eleven weeks for the series to un-
fold, seventy-seven days in which one
might forget how it began—a platoon
in transit, fatigued, the banality
of war, cast and crew billeted in this
very neighbourhood (and for much the same
duration) before I made it my home—
so that the sudden return to *the age
of Hooper*, the dismal reality
of troops moving on—a routine passage—
achieves an almost visceral recoil
that haunts me again: my boots in a crease
of trench-like mud; the glittering turmoil
that entranced me fast fading to a dream.

Brideshead Recorded

October, nineteen eighty-one.
It had only just begun
and we were off to Rhodes
so I set the VCR to tape
the two episodes

we'd miss, for our return—
from honeymoon—
to the altered shape
of our future lives, our routine.

The Gina Lollobrigida Method

for Michael James

Get the rhythm right—
lean in, and on
to the first beat
of the trill,
then ease off before
speeding through
the remaining,

        alternating notes.
        So you taught me
        like any good teacher
        by example, but
        it was something
        else, a playful
        mnemonic—

an exotic beauty
darting into my head—
that helped me replicate
your technique:
Gina Lollobrigida.
Now I too could
ripple my fingers

        to perfection
        whenever I saw
        the *tr* in the score.
        A wavy line
        might indicate
        an extension
        of the *lol*

or the *brig*,
but the simple trick
remained the same—
until, that is, I heard
of the sudden,
fatal haemorrhage
in your brain.

Now, what lingers
in my thoughts
as I play, is not only
that scintillating name
but also, more
bleakly, the unsettling
complication of *you*.

'When I'm 64'

Twelve months to go before
I reach the age my father
died; my wife already gone
at the same mean 58 as my mother;
three long years since the tune

lost much of its charm. But then
I still sing along, *bottle of wine...*
doing the garden...
Who could ask for more?

'When I'm 64' (Take 2)

The speculation will soon
be history, like 1984 or 2001,
though the simple tune
will still have its charm.
Perhaps there's just time

for me, yet again,
to send a *foolish Valentine*—
like Bathsheba Everdene.
Where would be the harm?

Saw

I find it by accident
in the shed, wrapped
in old newspaper
that's almost sepia,
the rusting
blade of a saw, whose
deep jagged wave

> gashes my palm.
> The headlines—from
> *The Daily Telegraph,*
> October 25, 1972—
> are confusingly torn,
> the saw having ripped
> through the news-

worthiness
of the news. A drop
in the pound *to $2.37...*
Fluoridation... Eva Peron...
CHIP SHOPS LOSE FIGHT...
though certain stories
are still intact:

> *Some anti-Market*
> *local authorities have*
> *declined to be involved in*
> *the "Fanfare for Europe"*
> *celebrations, but fifteen*
> *symphony orchestras*
> *are taking part.*

And as I read, it's as if
the line between fact
and fantasy is in tatters.
Will the England goalkeeper
regain his sight? And who
is telling me, below,
in the personal column:

> DARLING, *we've never met*
> *but we're so perfect*
> *for each other! Let*
> *Com-Pat*
> *Computer Dating*
> *introduce us now.*
> *01-437-4025.*

Beauty and the Beast

With every remake
the thorns are sharper,
the snowy forest
colder still.
Here, the harpsichord
is a trigger-happy maniac;
his wardrobe-wife opens

> to a full opera
> house—*La-la!*
> And though you are
> served by the same teapot
> chattering to her sidekick
> cup, and the poor clock,
> as ever, can't tell

the time,
there are now
real (scary!) people
and with one of them
you're obsessed.
Every night you gaze
upon her image you grow

> more haggard.
> You know the tunes
> by heart, but that
> won't save you. Wolves
> are on the loose
> as you face
> the magic mirror

and the truth: the beast
is always sacrificed
for the man who
thinks himself a prince,
despite the fact he's
wiser, warmer, more
companionable;

> most of all, he loves
> her the best—
> prepared to let her go.
> *I don't deserve you...*
> *It doesn't stop me longing...*
> *There may be something*
> *there that wasn't there before.*

[untitled]

I start well, and place
each fading memory
in my private museum
until faced with a real wretch,
surely best consigned
to oblivion—for which
I must create

      a whole new space.
      Here I can sense things
      long, long gone: awkward
      truths of how I first fed
      and rid my bowels of waste;
      formative skins shed
      to allow

for further growth.
How very useful! as now
I try to accommodate
the clash of pleasures
once held dear,
so familiar
through and through,

      with fresh imaginings:
      the intimate,
      breath-
      taking touch
      that thrills but spurns—
      the looming palimpsest
      of you and *you*.

In time
the sweetest dream
will have to make way too,
as my stumbling desire—
(though oh so very
gently) declined—
turns

        to pain, its final home
        this eery gallery
        of what doesn't exist,
        where ever more
        unreachable treasures
        quietly accumulate,
        gathering no dust.

Play it, Sam

Which always means *again*.
And the poor piano player
has no more choice
than the lover.
You must remember this,

A kiss is just a kiss...
There's only so much pain,
only so much time goes by
before you'll hit on Spotify.

Face the Music

It's rarely the dramatic drumroll
of dismissal, or the sound
of enemy gunfire
over the trench. It's more
likely the old TV quiz show

comes to mind before
everything you must atone for
moves in to take its toll,
muffled blow after blow.

Film Night

The evening we go out
to the cinema, the water
cuts off. You were set
to wash your hair,
over the bath, but
are suddenly unsure,
as we leave, which way

     to turn the tap.
     When we come back
     the house is in darkness;
     there's a waterfall across
     the stairwell, the dog
     trembling behind it
     with no idea anymore

how to welcome us
home. My violin case
is soggy cardboard
(the violin
miraculously intact);
water has poured
through the old analogue

     synth; and within a day
     my piano keys will warp
     to a mouldy waveform.
     It's years later,
     when I'm abroad,
     already with a sense
     of impending shock,

that my daughter
calls, telling me you've died—
on that same bathroom floor
where now, as I re-edit
these scenes in my head
as it seems I must,
I kneel and adjust

> the taps to mix warm
> water—just right—then
> gently work
> the soft, rich lather
> through your hair and rinse
> it off, for whatever further
> adventure we might enact.

High Fidelity

I can dim the lights and sing you songs full of sad things ...
I can serenade and gently play on your heart strings
        —Freddie Mercury

It came on the radio, just a few
lines, followed by other fragments; they were
raiding the songbook to tell the story
of his life.
                I was painting the ceiling
in the barn. You were miles away, the far
end, but you turned, smiling, and caught my eye.

Today, I'm in the same space, feeling lost...
same music on the stereo, hi–fi,
whatever it should now be called. A new
ceiling fan's in place, slowly revolving.

The night before your funeral, our two
daughters were up late, making a playlist.
And though I wished they'd get to bed, I knew
the need for their faithful inventory.

Recomposed

after Max Richter/Vivaldi

In my reimagined childhood I am
more like my grandson with three languages
aged five, not stumbling over my own name.
I now remember to meet my mother
at the gate to the park, at the right time.

And in this curious parallel world
there's an improvised feeling—it's the jazz
that in my former life I couldn't play.
I am a different kind of dreamer, my way-
ward impulse more constructively channelled,

treating the original with all due
respect and irreverence just the same.
I am fast becoming altogether
more like myself, believable, more true.

Afterword

In 1981 I was playing in a support band in Central Hall, York University, on an electric grand piano I was told had belonged to Charles Aznavour, writer of the song 'She' with lyricist Herbert Kretzmer. Little did I know that would be one of the songs chosen for my wife Clare's funeral, a few decades later. The details of that era—and further back—have been much in my thoughts while writing this book, together with dear friends now gone, of whom Clare is of course the most prominent.

The musical theme extends to other aspects of my experience—and preoccupations: music for film, my time at Winchester Cathedral, and my deep fascination with the maverick violinist, Nigel Kennedy. I hope this collection speaks to those who are moved by music of such diverse origins and styles, and readers for whom music is such an ally to poetry. Having suffered a physical injury that hampered my ability to play an instrument over the past year, poetry has been for me the perfect correspondent. And 'locked down' in Bulmer, idyllic setting though it may be, my thoughts have inevitably veered between the 'here and now' and the other locations that have a hold on me: Venice, Australia, and the past.

Apart from the prose poems, almost everything in this volume is derived in some way from the sonnet form, including miniature nine-liners (with a debt to Oliver Reynolds) and half-rhyming triple-deckers of 42 lines. These were a feature of my previous collection, *Chromatic*. I missed the launch of that book at the National Library in Canberra, needing to travel back to England for Clare's funeral, but the transcript of the launch speech by Melinda Smith told me the form should perhaps be known as the 'Munden'. I liked that—enough to let the form dominate this new book.

With thanks to Elvis Costello and Jeff Lynne, whose versions of 'She' have been invaluable companions.

Notes

'Greensleeves': Mantovani's house in Branksome Park, 'Greensleeves', is now marked by a blue heritage plaque.

Enfant Terrible: The boy/musician here is Nigel Kennedy. *The Boom of the Tingling Strings* is a piano concerto by Jon Lord (with whom Kennedy has played), its title taken from a phrase in the poem 'Piano' by DH Lawrence.

The Four Seasons: These versions of the original sonnets contained in Vivaldi's score are based on literal translations provided by Anouska Zummo. The project is discussed in a co-authored article:

www.textjournal.com.au/speciss/issue51/Munden&Zummo.pdf

Fractious: Nigel Kennedy's concert with the Detroit Symphony Orchestra eventually featured neither Elgar nor Ellington but his own 'Dedications' from the album *My World* (2016).

Duet: The Wilfred Owen and Siegfried Sassoon violins were made by Steve Burnett in honour of the two poets and their lost generation. The poem (commissioned by ArchiCantiores) was read (and the violin played) at Wilfred Owen's grave side in Ors, northern France, on the centenary of his death.

Don't look now: The film referenced was adapted from a Daphne du Maurier story and directed by Nicholas Roeg (1973).

From *The Wreck of the Unbelievable:* Damien Hirst's exhibition, 'Treasures from the Wreck of the Unbelievable', was staged across two venues in Venice, 2017.

Vaudeville: 'Winchester Cathedral', by Geoff Stephens, was performed on tour in the US and UK by the specially formed New Vaudeville Band. The BBC Light Programme was replaced by Radios 1 and 2 in 1967.

White Noise: The adapted quotations are from William Wordsworth, 'Lines Composed a Few Miles above Tintern Abbey' and Robert Lowell, 'For John Berryman'.

Sound Effects: The Yamaha FS1-E, affectionately known as the 'Fizzy' was a popular 50cc motorcycle of the 1970s.
Sam Peckinpah's abandoned adaptation of *Castaway*, the novella by James Gould Cozzens, is the focus of Paul Munden's screenplay, *Six Mile Creek*, in development.

'Assuming Equilibrium': Jerry Fielding was a regular composer for Sam Peckinpah, winning an Oscar nomination for his music to *The Wild Bunch*, but his score for *The Getaway* was replaced at Steve McQueen's insistence. Gordon Dawson described the subtlety of Fielding's score as 'like a man in a green suit walking in a forest'.

The Romantics: These prose poems were written as part of a collaborative prose poetry project with Cassandra Atherton, Paul Hetherington and Jen Webb, focusing on intertext and ekphrasis.

Niccolò Paganini: 'The Battle of Bloody Porch' is the name given to the climactic scene of Sam Peckinpah's film, *The Wild Bunch* (1969).

Frédéric Chopin: 'The Stones in the Park', a free concert by the Rolling Stones in Hyde Park, 1969, took on an unexpected mood after the death of their guitarist, Brian Jones, two days earlier.

Richard Wagner: Alma Mahler was the original subject of the phrase, 'the loveliest girl in Vienna'.

Arthur Sullivan: Sullivan's 'The Lost Chord' is based on a poem by Adelaide Anne Procter.

Camille Saint-Saëns: Saint-Saëns' theme from his Symphony No. 3 is used in the song 'If I had Words' by Scott Fitzgerald, released in 1978.

Claude Debussy: Debussy's *Claire de Lune* is based on Paul Verlaine's poem of the same title. William Walker was a diver who shored up Winchester Cathedral over a period of five years, 1906–1911. 'A Nightingale Sang in Berkeley Square' was written by Manning Sherwin, with lyrics by Eric Maschwitz. The title was taken from a story in Michael Arlen's 1923 collection, *These Charming People*.

Engelbert Humperdink, aka Arnold 'Gerry' Dorsey, came 25th out of 26 in the Eurovision Song Contest, 2012. His hit 'Release Me' had spent 56 weeks in the top 50, 1967–8. He is still touring. Paul Munden and Kit

Monkman were due to work with Adrian Wagner on television music in 1991. Their new film, *The Darkroom*, is in development.

Antonín Dvořák: The central quotation is from Kenneth Grahame's *The Wind in the Willows* (1908). Ridley Scott's 1973 Hovis advert was remastered and screened again in 2019.

Maurice Ravel: Ravel's *Pavane* was adapted as a popular song by Peter DeRose and Bert Shefter, with lyrics by Mitchell Parish. Ravel's piano suite *Gaspard de la nuit* (1909) is based on the prose poem collection by Aloysius Bertrand. Cassandra Atherton is (or was) a keen skater.

Jean Sibelius: Roger Waters staged a version of Pink Floyd's *The Wall* in Berlin on 21 July 1990. Paul Hetherington and Bruce Willis have never been seen in the same room.

Sergei Rachmaninoff: Rachmaninoff left Russia after the revolution, finally settling in Beverly Hills in 1942.

Alma Mahler Gropius Werfel: Visconti's *Death in Venice* is based on Thomas Mann's novel of the same name. Alban Berg dedicated his violin concerto (codedly) to Manon Gropius. It makes use of Bach's chorale, 'Es ist genug'.

Sir William Harris was appointed assistant organist at St David's, Wales, in 1897, aged 14. Clement McWilliam, for several years sub-organist at Winchester Cathedral, was assistant to William Harris at the Royal Chapel, Windsor, 1959, the year Clare Elizabeth Mallorie Munden was born.

Slowly, Quietly: The 'biennale' tortoises were at the Seychelles International Airport for two weeks, after which they moved to the Eden Art Space gallery, for sale.

'When I'm 64': The song referenced is by Lennon and McCartney (presumably all McCartney), recorded in 1966.

Saw: A car crash in October 1972 cost the England goalkeeper Gordon Banks the sight in his right eye.

Beauty and the Beast: The closing lines are taken from Disney's 2017 live-action remake of the earlier animated film.

Play it, Sam: The 1931 song referenced, 'As Time Goes By', is by Herman Hupfeld and is used in the film *Casablanca* (dir. Curtiz, 1942).

Recomposed: The title derives from the Deutsche Grammophon project, notably Vivaldi—The Four Seasons, Recomposed by Max Richter (2012).

Acknowledgements

Some of the poems in this collection have previously appeared in journals and anthologies: *Abstractions, ACT States of Poetry Anthology (Series Three), Alcatraz, Axon: Creative Explorations, The Canberra Times, Empty House: Poetry and Prose on the Climate Crisis, Giant Steps, Metamorphic: 21st century poets respond to Ovid, The Stony Thursday Book, Western Humanities Review.*

Versions of several prose poem sequences were included in the Authorised Theft chapbook sets: *Colours, Prosody, The Six Senses, C19: Intertext/Ekphrasis.*

Some poems have also been displayed within University of Canberra staff exhibitions: *The Uncertainty Principle* (ANCA Gallery, 2018), *[dash]topia* (ANCA Gallery, 2019), *On Forgetting* (Belconnen Arts Centre, 2021).

With thanks to Paul Hetherington and Oliver Comins for their invaluable advice on redrafting some of the poems.

About the author

Paul Munden is a poet, editor and screenwriter living in North Yorkshire. A Gregory Award winner, he has published five poetry collections, including *Analogue/Digital: New & Selected Poems* (Smith|Doorstop, 2015), *The Bulmer Murder* (RWP, 2017) and *Chromatic* (UWA Publishing, 2017), and six prose poetry chapbooks. He is editor (or co-editor) of various anthologies, including *Metamorphic: 21st century poets respond to Ovid* (RWP, 2017) and *Divining Dante* (RWP, 2021), and is the current poetry editor of *Westerly Magazine*. For the British Council he has covered a number of scientific and humanitarian themes, as conference poet, and edited the anthology, *Feeling the Pressure: Poetry and science of climate change* (British Council, 2008). He was director of the UK's National Association of Writers in Education, 1994-2018, and is now a Royal Literary Fund Fellow at the University of Leeds. He is also an Adjunct Associate Professor at the University of Canberra, Australia, where he established the 'Poetry on the Move' festival. Having worked throughout the 1990s as reader for Stanley Kubrick, he has recently returned to the world of film as writer and co-developer of adapted and original screenplays.

Ingram Content Group UK Ltd.
Milton Keynes UK
UKHW011950020723
424412UK00001B/10